Weeds and Wildings, chiefly :
With
a Rose or Two

Weeds and Wildings, chiefly :
With
a Rose or Two

By H. M.

'Alms for oblivion'

'Youth is the proper, permanent and genuine
condition of man."
— Nathanial Hawthorne

'Yes, decay is often a gardener,' — Anonymous

Micro Publishing Media, Inc.
PO Box 1522, Stockbridge, MA 01262
or
Deborah@micropublishingmedia.com

www.micropublishingmedia.info
www.melvillepress.com

ISBN 978-1-944068-14-1

Melville Press
a Division of Micro Publishing Media, Inc.

Printed in the United States of America

CLOVER

'Ye field flowers ! the garden's eclipse you, 'tis true,
Yet wildings of Nature, I dote upon you.'
— Campbell

CREDITS

Cover etching by Claire Illouz; property of the Berkshire County Historical Society; used by permission of the artist.

Research and editing by J. Peter Bergman.

Cover and book design by Jane McWhorter

Photographs used with permission from the Berkshire Athenaeum, Melville Collection; Kathleen Reilly, director.

Manuscript reproductions from the Melville collection at Harvard University – Houghton Library, Cambridge, Mass; with permission; thank you, Dennis Marnon.

Previous published editions consulted for this volume:

The Works of Herman Melville, Volume 8: Poems, edited by Raymond Weaver; Constable and Company LTD, 1924.

Collected Poems of Herman Melville, edited by Howard P. Vincent; Packard/ Hendricks House, Chicago, 1947.

Tales, Poems and Other Writings, edited by John Bryant, The Modern Library Classics, 2002.

Selected Poems of Herman Melville, edited by Hennig Cohen; Fordham University Press, 1991.

and

The Melville Log: A Documentary Life of Herman Melville, 1819-1891, edited by Jay Leyda; Harcourt, Brace, New York, 1951.

Herman Melville, revised edition, by Tyrus Hillway, edited by Sylvia E. Bowman; Twayne's United States Authors Series, 1979.

Herman Melville, A to Z, Carl Rollyson and Lisa Paddock, Checkmark Books, 2001.

Herman Melville, A Biography by Hershel Parker; John Hopkins University Press, 1996.

Thank you to Elizabeth Sherman, Deborah Herman, Jeff Herman and all who encouraged this project.

INTRODUCTION

In 1890 Herman Melville was collecting, for a gift to his wife Elizabeth Knapp Shaw Melville, a group of late works that would be published privately—in a very limited edition—as *Weeds and Wildings, chiefly; With a Rose or Two*. It would consist of new pieces and other poems written much earlier that had never before seen the light of day. Many of them clearly refer to plants, birds and animals that were seen at Arrowhead, his home in The Berkshires where he had written the final draft of Moby-Dick; or, The Whale in the winter of 1850-1851. Ill with erysipelas (a painful inflammation of the skin) and aging, he was also trying to finish a new, lengthy story entitled Billy Budd, Sailor which told the morality tale of abuse and restraint, his best delineation of pure evil versus pure good. Not since his whaling novel had he embraced with such clarity that eternal struggle.

According to biographer Hershel Parker, "both sections [of the poetry collection] . . . portray a man content to acknowledge that he 'came to his roses late' but not too late, and content to celebrate spousal love in old age." At the time of his 44th wedding anniversary in August, 1891 he was still working on the book, revising the order of poems and moving its sections around to get the effect he desired. He had included a reconceiving of the classic story, Rip van Winkle in the collection as well, along with a dedication to "Winnefred" a nickname for his wife, Lizzie, which in Welsh is spelled Guinevere (wife of King Arthur) and means 'blessed reconciliation, or friend of peace.' In the Scots variation the name becomes Úna meaning 'one', as in the Edmund Spenser epic poem "The Faerie Queene" (1590, 1596), where the Anglicized name is borne by a beautiful female character. Melville, ever the avid reader and scholar, reflects his family's Scottish heritage in the choice of nickname for Lizzie at this stage of their long and difficult relationship, a marriage marred by mental health issues and financial difficulties.

In this book he lauded red clover as one of the "dearest flowers of the field" describing both red and white as symbolic of the couple's time to-gether at Arrowhead where they were not exactly "Living in clover." He refers to his brother Allan, who took over the ownership of Herman and

Lizzie's home as "the urbane barbarian" whose misuse of the property he disdains, thereby speaking ill of the dead. In Melville's memory of events he comments on the snow on the leaves of his weeds and wildings (defined as wild things) as "tears of the happy," a phrase Lizzie had coined which now referred more to his own bittersweet memories than to the dew-like afterlife of nature's moisture on those leaves.

Herman never got over the loss of the home he created for his growing family; the place where he planned to grow old with his favorite chimney hearth, where he had foreseen a glorious life as famous author and gentleman farmer. By the time he had his collection of poems and stories ready to present to "Winnefred," he was old, ill, lost in memories and struggling to finish his final masterwork. He opened his book with the poem, "Clover" as part of the extended memory he cites in the dedication and ends it with "Wiser in relish, if sedate, / Come graybeards to their roses late." It was late for Melville, certainly, who died on September 28, 1891 with this book as his instant legacy, though seen by very few. It was a reward, however, for his faithful and loving widow, an apology of sorts for the difficulties of their time together.

There are variations in the order of poems beginning with his earliest listing of them on February 13, 1890 (see below, as published in The Melville Log) through the last publication of the complete collection in 1947, edited by Howard P. Vincent. This collection reflects Melville's original intent with a few alterations. Instead of two sections (AS THEY FELL Part 1st A Rose or Two, and Part 2nd Weeds and Wildings) there are five distinct sections with the Rip Van Winkle story/poem taking its own single place in the center of the collection. With the publisher's and designer's advice I have renumbered the final sections of the book. Originally A ROSE OR TWO was the title for the groups of poems that ended the book with Part I being AS THEY TELL and Part II being THE ROSE FARMER which included the last poem L'ENVOI. We have chose for clarity in content to call these sections PART IV-AS THEY TELL - A ROSE OR TWO and PART V – THE ROSE FARMER. In both *Weeds and Wildings* and the uncollected poems appended at the end of the book Vincent often uses variant forms of the poems and alternate word choices in key spots. I have chosen to use the versions that make the most sense when read aloud.

J. Peter Bergman
Arrowhead, October, 2015

As They Fell

Part 1st A Rose or Two

From Beads for a Rosary
The Rose Entombed
[The] New Rosecrucians
Hearth Roses
[The] Vial of Attar
The Ambuscade
Under the Snow
Amoroso
Ch[ancel?] Rose ["The Accepted Time"?]
[The] Rose Window
The Devotion of the Flowers to their Lady
Roses of Damascus [alternate title: "The Rose Farmer"]
L'Envoi

Part 2d Weeds & Wildings (Wild Things)

Murder will out [title altered to: "Time's Betrayal"]
[The] Old Ship[master and His Crazy Barn]
Vine & Goat
Old Rainbow
Profundity & Levity
Inscription for Rip Van Winkle
Lonie [title altered by Elizabeth Melville to: "Shadow
The Cuban Pirate   at the Feast"]
Madcap's Ditty [former title: "Wild-Strawberry Hunters"]
The Avatar
[The] American Aloe [on Exhibition]
Iris [MS dated by Elizabeth Melville: 1874]
A Ground Vine [intercedes with the Queen of Flowers for
                          the merited Recognition of Clover]

CLOVER DEDICATION
TO
WINNEFRED

With you and me, Winnie, Red Clover has always been one of the dearest of the flowers of the field : an avowal— by the way—as you well ween, which implies no undelight as to this ruddy young brother's demure half-sister, White Clover. Our feeling for both sorts originates in no fanciful associations egotistic in kind. It is not, for example, because in any exceptional way we have verified in experience the aptness of that pleasant figure of speech, Living in clover— not for this do we so take the Ruddy One, for all that we once dwelt annually surrounded by flushed acres of it. Neither have we, jointly or severally, so frequently lighted upon that rare four-leaved variety accounted of happy augury to the finder ; though, to be sure, on my part, I yearly remind you of the coincidence in my chancing on such a specimen by the wayside on the early forenoon of the fourth day of a certain bridal month, now four years more than four times ten years ago.

But, tell, do we not take to this flower—for flower it is, though with the florist hardly ranking with the floral clans— not alone that in itself it is a thing of freshness and beauty, but also that being no delicate foster-child of the nurseryman, but a hardy little creature of out-of-doors accessible and familiar to every one, no one can monopolise its charm. Yes, we are communists here.

Sweet in the mouth of that brindled heifer, whose breath you so loved to inhale, and doubtless pleasant to the nostril and eye ; sweet as well to the like senses in ourselves ; prized by that most radical of men, the farmer to whom wild amaranths in a pasture, though emblems of immortality, are but weeds and anathema ; finding favour even with so peevish a busybody as the bee ; is it not the felicitous fortune of our favourite to incur no creature's displeasure, but to enjoy, and without striving for it, the spontaneous goodwill of all ? Why it is that this little peasant of the flowers revels in so enviable an immunity and privilege, not in equal degree shared by any of us mortals however gifted and good ; that indeed is something the reason whereof may not slumber very deep. But—In pace ; always leave a sleeper to his repose.

How often at our adopted homestead on the hillside—now ours no more—the farm house, long ago shorn by the urbane barbarian succeeding us in the proprietorship—shorn of its gambrel roof and dormer windows, and when I last saw it indolently setting in serene contentment of natural decay ; how often, Winnie, did I come in from my ramble early in the bright summer mornings of old, with a handful of these cheap little cheery roses of the meek newly purloined from the fields to consecrate them on that bit of a maple-wood mantel—your altar, somebody called it—in the familiar room facing your beloved South! And in October most did I please myself in gathering them from the moist matted aftermath in an enriched little hollow near by, soon to be snowed upon and for consecutive months sheeted from view. And once—you remember it—having culled them in a sunny little flurry of snow, winter's frolic skirmisher in advance, the genial warmth of your chamber melted the fleecy flakes into dewdrops rolling off from the ruddiness. 'Tears of the happy,' you said.

Well, and to whom but to thee, Madonna of the Trefoil, should I now dedicate these 'Weeds and Wildings,' thriftless children of quite another and yet later spontaneous after-growth, and bearing indications too apparent it may be, of that terminating season on which the offerer verges. But that any may possibly betray, call to mind the dissolved snow-flakes on the ruddy oblation of old, and remember your 'Tears of the Happy.'

Melville, in the manuscript, has written in pencil *Lizzie*—his wife's name—next to the name Winnefred indicating that he is dedicating this book to her.

CONTENTS

*indicates a poem not in the final manuscript

Weeds & Wildings

including chiefly:

A few flowers and buds

with

A Rose a Tree

" Man is the proper proper servant
and faun couldn of man"

by

HM.

Harvard University – Houghton Library / Melville, Herman, 1819–1891. Unpublished poems : autograph manuscript, undated. Herman Melville paper, 1761–1964. MS Am 188 (369.1). Houghton Library,Harvard University, Cambridge, Mass.

PART 1—THE YEAR

CLOVER

The June day dawns, the joy-winds rush,
    Your jovial fields are dresst ;
Rosier for thee the Dawn's red flush,
    Ruddier the Ruddock's breast.

THE LATE-COMER
[THE LOITERER]

She will come tho' she loiter, believe ;
Her pledge it assigns not the day ;
Why brood by the embers night after night
Sighing over their dying away—

Well, let her delay !
She is everywhere longed for as here,
She's a favourite, errant and young,
And we, we are fixtures and gray ;
Her can we gladden, though us she can cheer ?
Then let her delay !

But ah, can she think it no wrong.
When we pine but her footprints to see,
To tarry with the Prince of the South so long
Who prizes her less than we ?

But watch and wait.
Where southward our valley grows wide and
    great,
Somebody is peering in view,
Yes, up by the river-side way
The old path tracing anew :—

Along the banks by meadow-beds
Aslope to morning's ray ;
And, in distance timing the measure tone,
Garlanded one in her footing
A rosier foot on her footprint treads
And follows her night and day.

Then watch and wait :
Wait by the pasture-bars
Or watch by the garden gate ;
For, after coming, tho' wide she stray,
First ever she shows on the slender way—
Slim sheep-track threading the hill-side brown,
Or foot-path that leads to the garden down.

While snow lingered under the fir,
Loth to melt from embrace of the earth,
And ashy, red embers of logs
In moonlight dozed on the hearth ;
And in cage by the window sun-warmed
Our bird was enheartened to song ;
It was then that, as yearly before,
By the selfsame foot-path along,
She drew to the weather-bent door
That was sunned thro' the skeleton tree :

Nothing she said, but seemed to say—
'Old folks, aren't ye glad to see *me* ! '
And tears filled our eyes—bless the day !
Then she turned ; and where was she not ?
She was here—she was there,
Peeping eagerly everywhere
Like one who revisits scenes never forgot.

TIME'S BETRAYAL
[MURDER WILL OUT]

The tapping of a mature maple for the syrup, however recklessly
done, does not necessarily kill it. No ; since being an aboriginal child
of Nature, it is doubtless blessed with a constitution enabling it to
withstand a good deal of hard usage. But to bleed the immature
trunk, though some sugar-makers, detected in the act on ground not
their own, aver that it does the sylvan younker a deal of good, can
hardly contribute to the tree's amplest development, or, ensure the
patriarchal long life to it. Certain it is, that in some young maples the
annual tapping would seem to make precocious the autumnal ripen-
ing or change of the leaf. And such premature change would seem
strikingly to enhance the splendor of the tints.

Someone, whose morals need mending,
Sallies forth like the pillaging bee ;
He waylays the syrup ascending
In anyone's saccharine tree ;
So lacking in conscience indeed,
So reckless what life he makes bleed,
That to get at the juices, his staple,
The desirable sweets of the Spring,
He poignards a shapely young maple,
In my second-growth coppice—its king.
Assassin ! secure in a crime never seen,
The underwood dense, e'en his victim a screen,
So be. But the murder will out,
Never doubt, never doubt ;
In season the leafage will tell,
Turning red ere the rime
Yet, in turning, all beauty excel
For a time, for a time !
Small thanks to the scamp. But in vision, to me
A goddess mild painting the glorified tree
'So they change who die early, some bards who
      life render :
Keats, stabbed by the Muses, his garland's a
      splendour ! '

THE OLD SHIPMASTER
AND
HIS CRAZY BARN

Bewrinkled in shingle, and lichened in board,
With sills settling down to the sward,
My old barn it leaneth awry ;
It sags, and the wags wag their heads going by.

In March winds it creaks,
Each gaunt timber shrieks
Like ribs of a craft off Cape Horn ;
And in midst of the din
The foul weather beats in ;
And the grain-chest—'twould mould any corn !

Pull it down, says a neighbour.
Never mine be that labour !
For a Spirit inhabits, a fellowly one,
The like of which never responded to me
From the long hills and hollows that make up the sea,
Hills and hollows where Echo is none.

The site should I clear, and rebuild,
Would that Voice reinhabit ?—Self-willed,
Says each pleasing thing
Never Dives can buy,
Let me keep where I cling !
I am touchy as cinder
Yea, quick to take wing,
Nor return if I fly.

WHEN FORTH THE SHEPHERD
LEADS THE FLOCK

When forth the shepherd leads the flock,
White lamb and dingy ewe,
And there's dibbling in the garden,
Then the world begins anew.
When buttercups make bright
The meadows up and down,
The Golden Age returns to fields
If never to the town.
When stir the freshening airs
Forerunning showers to meads,
And Dandelions prance,
Then Heart-Free shares the dance—
A Wilding with the Weeds !
    But alack and alas
    For things of wilding feature !
    Since hearsed was Pan
    Ill befalls each creature—
    Profitless to man !

Buttercup and Dandelion
Wildings, and the rest,
Commoners and holiday-makers
Note them in one test :

The farmers scout them,
Yea, and would rout them,
Hay is better without them—
Tares in the grass !
The florists pooh-pooh them ;
Few but children do woo them,
Love them, reprieve them,
Retrieve and inweave them,
Never sighing—*Alas* !

THE LITTLE GOOD-FELLOWS

Make way, make way, give leave to rove
Your orchard under as above :
A yearly welcome if ye love !
And all who loved us always throve.

Love for love. For ever we
When some unfriended man we see
Lifeless under forest-eaves,
Cover him with buds and leaves ;
And charge the chipmunk, mouse, and mole—
Molest not this poor human soul !

Then let us never on green floor
Where your paths wind roundabout,
Keep to the middle in misdoubt,
Shy and aloof, unsure of ye ;
But come like grass to stones on moor
Fearless wherever mortals be.

But toss your caps, O maids and men,
Snow-bound long in farm-house pen :
We chase Old Winter back to den.
See our red waistcoats ! Alive be then—
Alive to the bridal-favours when
They blossom in your orchards every Spring,
And cock-robin curves on a bridegroom's
     wing !

THE OLD FASHION

Now youthful is Ver
And the same, and forever
Year after year ;
And her bobolinks sing,
And they vary never
In juvenile cheer.

Old-fashioned is Ver
Tho' eternally new,
And her bobolink's young
Keep the old fashion true :
Chee, Chee ! they will sing
While the welkin is blue.

MADCAPS

Through the orchard I follow
Two children in glee.
From an apple-tree's hollow
They startle the bee.

The White Clover throws
Perfume in their way
    To the hedge of Red Rose ;
Between Roses and Clover
The Strawberry grows.
It is Lily and Cherry
Companioned by Butterflies
Madcaps as merry !

BUTTERFLY DITTY

Summer comes in like a sea,
Wave upon wave how bright ;
Thro' the heaven of summer we'll flee
And tipple the light !

From garden to garden,
Such charter have we,
We'll rove and we'll revel,
And idlers we'll be !

We'll rove and we'll revel,
Concerned but for this—
That man, Eden's bad boy,
Partakes not the bliss.

THE BLUEBIRD

Beneath yon Larkspur's azure bells
That sun their bees in balmy air
In mould no more the Blue-Bird dwells
Tho' late he found interment there.

All stiff he lay beneath the Fir
When shrill the March piped overhead,
And Pity gave him sepulchre
Within the Garden's sheltered bed.

And soft she sighed—Too soon he came;
On wings of hope he met the knell ;
His heavenly tint the dust shall tame ;
Ah, some misgivings had been well !

But, look, the clear ethereal hue
In June it makes the Larkspur's dower;
It is the self-same welkin-blue—
The Bird's transfigured in the Flower.

THE LOVER
AND
THE SYRINGA-BUSH

Like a lit-up Christmas Tree,
Like grotto pranked with spars,
Like white corals in green sea,
Like night's sky of crowded stars—
To me like these you show, Syringa,
Such heightening power has love, believe,
While here by Eden's gate I linger
Love's tryst to keep with truant Eve.

THE DAIRYMAN'S CHILD

Soft as the morning
When South winds blow,
Sweet as the peach-orchards
When blossoms are seen,
Pure as a fresco
Of roses and snow
Or an opal serene.

TROPHIES OF PEACE
[ILLINOIS IN 1840]

Files on files of prairie maize :
On hosts of spears the morning plays !
Aloft the rustling streamers show :
The floss embrowned is rich below.

When Asia scarfed in silks came on
Against the Greek and Marathon,
Did each plume and pennon dance
Sun-lit thus on helm and lance
Mindless of War's sickle so ?

For them, a tasselled dance of death :
For these—the reapers reap them low,
Reap them low and stack the plain
With Ceres' trophies, golden grain.

Such monuments, and only such,
O Prairie ! termless yield,
Though trooper Mars disdainful flout
Nor Annals fame the field.

IN THE PAUPER'S TURNIP-FIELD

Crow, in pulpit lone and tall
Of yon charred hemlock, grimly dead,
Why on me in preachment call—
Me, by nearer preachment led
Here in homily of my hoe.
The hoe, the hoe,
My heavy hoe
That earthward bows me to foreshow
A mattock heavier than the hoe.

A WAYSIDE WEED

By orchards red he whisks along,
A charioteer from the villa fine ;
With passing lash o' the whip he cuts
A Way-side Weed divine.

But know he what it is he does ?
He flouts October's god
Whose scepter is this Way-side Weed,
This swaying Golden Rod ?

THE CHIPMUNK

Heart of autumn !
        Weather meet,
Like to sherbert
        Cool and sweet.
Stock-still I stand,
        And him I see
Prying, peeping
        From the Beech-tree ;
Crickling, crackling
        Gleefully !

But, affrighted
        By wee sound,
Presto ! vanish—
        Whither bound ?

So did Baby,
        Crowing mirth,
E'en as startled
By some inkling
        Touching Earth,
Flit (and whither ?)
        From our hearth !

MICHAELMAS DAISIES
FIELD ASTERS UNDER MICHAELMAS DAISIES

Like the stars in commons blue
Peep their namesakes, Asters here,
Wild ones every autumn seen—
Seen of all, arresting few.

Seen indeed. But who their cheer
Interpret may, or what they mean,
When so inscrutably their eyes
No star-gazers scrutinise.

STOCKINGS IN
THE FARM-HOUSE CHIMNEY

Happy, believe, this Christmas Eve
Are Willie and Rob and Nellie and May—
Happy in hope ! in hope to receive
These stockings well stuffed from Santa Claus'
          sleigh.

O the delight to believe in a wight
More than the mortal, with something of man,
Whisking about, an invisible sprite ?
Almoner blest of Oberon's clan.

Stay, Truth, O stay in a long delay !
Why should these little ones find you out ?
Let them forever with fable play,
Evermore hang the stocking out !

ALWAYS WITH US !—
THE BLACK PREACHER

Betimes a wise guest
His visit will sever,
Yes, absence endears.
Revisit he would,
So remains not forever.

Well, Robin, the wise one
He went yestreen,
Bound for the South
Where his chums convene.

Back, he'll come back
In his new Spring vest
And the more for his absence
Be welcomed with zest.

But thou, black Crow,
Inconsiderate fowl,
Wilt never away—
Take elsewhere thy cowl ?

From the blasted hemlock's
Whitened spur
Whatever the season,
Or Winter or Ver
Or Summer or Fall,
Croaker, foreboder,
We hear thy call—
Caw ! Caw ! Caw !

A DUTCH CHRISTMAS UP THE HUDSON
IN THE TIME OF PATROONS

Over the ruddy hearth, lo, the green bough !
In house of the sickle and home of the plough,
Arboured I sit and toast apples now !

Hi, there in barn ! have done with the flail,
Worry not the wheat, nor winnow in the gale :
'Tis Christmas and holiday, turkey, too, and ale !

Creeping round the wainscot of old oak red
The ground-pine, see—smell the sweet balsam shed !

Leave off, Katrina, to tarry there and scan :
The cream will take its time, girl, to rise in the pan.
Meanwhile here's a knocking, and the caller it is *Van*,
Tuenis Van der Benmacher, your merry Christmas
        man.

Leafless the grove now where birds billed the kiss :
To-night when the fiddler wipes his forehead, I wis,
And panting from the dance come our Hans and
        Cousin Chris,
Yon bush in the window will never be amiss !

But oats have ye heaped, men, for horses in stall ?
And for each heifer young and old mother-cow
Have ye raked down the hay from the aftermath-
        mow ?
The Christmas let come to the creatures one and all !

Tho' the pedlar, peering in, doubtless deemed it but
        folly,
The yoke-cattle's horns did I twine with green holly.

Good to breathe their sweet breath this blest Christmas
      morn,
Mindful of the ox, ass, and Babe new-born.

The snow drifts and drifts, and the frost it benumbs :
Elsie, pet, scatter to the snow-birds your crumbs.

Sleigh-bells a' jingle ! 'Tis Santa Claus : hail !
Villageward he goes thro' the spooming of the snows ;
Yes, hurrying to round his many errands to a close,
A mince-pie he's taking to the one man in jail,—
What ! drove right out between the gate-posts here ?
Well, well, little Sharp-Eyes, blurred panes we must
      clear !

Our Santa Claus a clever way has and a free :
Gifts from him some will take who would never take
      from me ;
For poor hereabouts there are none—none so poor
But that pudding for an alms they would spurn from
      the door.

All the same to all in the world's wide ways,
Happy harvest of the conscience on many Christmas
      Days.

MY JACKET OLD

My jacket old, with narrow seam—
When the dull day's work is done
I dust it, and of Asia dream,
Old Asia of the sun !
There other garbs prevail ;
Yea, lingering there, free robe and vest,
Edenic Leisure's age attest,
Ere work, alack came in with Wail.

IN THE OLD FARM-HOUSE
THE GHOST

Dead of night, dead of night,
    Living souls are abed ;
Dead of night, dead of night,
    And I sit with the dead.

He laughs in white sheet,
    And I, I laugh too,
'Tis Shakespeare—good fellow—
    And Falstaff in view.

A BATTLE PICTURE

Three mounted buglers laced in gold,
    Sidelong veering, light in seat,
High on the crest of battle rolled
    Ere yet the surge is downward beat,
Their pennoned trumpets lightly hold,
    Mark how they snatch the swift occasion
    To thrill their rearward invocation,
While the sabres, never coy,
    Ring responses as they ride ;
And, like breakers of the tide,
    All the mad plumes dance for joy !

PART II – THIS, THAT AND THE OTHER

PROFUNDITY AND LEVITY

An owl in his wonted way-long retirement ruffled by the meadowlark curveting and carolling in the morning sun high over the pastures and woods, comments upon that rollicker, and in so doing lets out the meditation engrossing him when thus molested. But the weightiness of the wisdom ill agrees with the somewhat thrilling expression ; an incongruity attributable doubtless to the contagious influence of the reprehended malapert's overruling song :—

So frolic, so flighty.
Leaving wisdom behind ;
Lark, little you ween
Of the progress of mind.

While fantastic you're winging,
Upcurving and singing,
A skylarking dot in the sun ;
Under eaves here in wood
My wits am I giving
To this latest theme ;
Life blinks at strong light,
Life wanders in night like a dream—
Is life then worth living ?

INSCRIPTION

For a boulder near the spot where the last Hardhack was laid low by the new proprietor of the Hill of Arrowhead.

A weed grew here. Exempt from use,
Weeds turn no wheel, nor run ;
Radiance pure or redolence
Some have, but this had none,
And yet heaven gave it leave to live
And idle it in the sun.

THE CUBAN PIRATE

*(Some of the more scintillant West Indian humming-birds
are in frame hardly bigger than a beetle or bee.)*

Buccaneer in gemmed attire—
Ruby, amber, emerald, jet—
Darkling, sparkling dot of fire
Still on plunder are you set?

Summer is your sea, and there
The flowers afloat you board and ravage,
Yourself a thing more dazzling fair—
Tiny, plummed, bejeweled Savage !

Midget ! yet in passion fell
Furioso, Creoles tell.
Wing'd are you Cupid in disguise
Now flying spark of Paradise ?

THE RUSTY MAN

(BY A SOURED ONE)

In La Mancha he mopeth,
    With beard thin and dusty ;
He doteth and mopeth
    In Library fusty—
'Mong his old folios gropeth :
    Cities' obsolete saws
    Of chivalry's laws—
    Be the wronged one's knight :
    Die, but do right.
So he rusts and he musts,
While each grocer green
Thrives apace with the fulsome face
Of a fool serene.

A SPIRIT APPEARED TO ME

A spirit appeared to me, and said
' Where now would you choose to dwell ?
In the Paradise of the Fool
Or in wise Solomon's hell ? '

Never he asked me twice :
' Give me the Fool's Paradise. '

THE AMERICAN ALOE ON EXHIBITION

It is but a floral superstition, as everybody knows, that
this plant flowers only once in a century. When in any
instance the flowering is for decades delayed beyond the
normal period (eight or ten years at farthest), it is owing to
something retarding in the environment or soil.

But few they were who came to see
The Century-Plant in flower :
Ten cents admission—price you pay
For bon-bons of the hour.

In strange inert blank unconcern
Of wild things at the Zoo,
The patriarch let the sight-seers stare—
These seldom more than two.

But lone at night the garland sighed,
And while moaned the aged stem :
'At last, at last ! but joy and pride
What part have I with them ? '

Let be the dearth that kept me back
Now long from wreath decreed ;
But, ah, ye Roses that have passed
Accounting me a weed !

TIME'S LONG AGO !

Time's Long Ago ! Nor coral isles
In the blue South Sea more serene,
When the lagoons unruffled show,
There Fates and Furies change their mien.
Though strewn with wreckage be the shore,
The halcyon haunts it ; all is green
And wins the heart that hope can lure no more.

FRUIT AND FLOWER PAINTER

She dens in a garret
     As void as a drum ;
In lieu of plum-pudding—
     She paints the plum !

     No use in my grieving,
         The shops I must suit :
     Broken hearts are not potsherds—
         Paint flowers and fruit !

How whistles her garret,
     A sieve for the snows :
She hums *Si fortuna*,
     And—paints the rose !

     December is howling,
         But feign it a flute   ;
     Help on the deceiving—
         Paint flowers and fruit !

PART III—RIP VAN WINKLE'S LILAC *

TO

A HAPPY SHADE

Under the golden maples where there now reclinest, sharing Fame's
Indian Summer with those mellowing Immortals who as men were
not only excellent in their works, but pleasant and love-worthy in
their lives ; little troublest thou thyself, O Washington Irving, as to
who peradventure may be poaching in that literary manor which
thou leftest behind. Still less is it thou, happy Shade, that will charge
with presumption the endeavor to render something tributary to the
story of that child of thy heart—Rip Van Winkle. For aught I, or
anybody, knows to the contrary, thy vision may now be such that it
may even reach here where I write, and thy spirit be pleased to behold
me inspired by whom but thyself.

RIP VAN WINKLE

Riverward emerging towards sunset in leafy June from
a dark clove or gorge of the Kattskills, dazed with his
long sleep in an innermost hollow of those mountains,
the good-natured good-for-nothing comes to an upland
pasture. Hearing his limping footfall in the loneliness,
the simpletons of young steers, there left to themselves
for the summer, abruptly lifting their heads from the
herbage stand as stupefied with astonishment while he
passes. In farther descent he comes to a few raggedly
cultivated fields detached and apart ; but no house as
yet, and presently strikes a wood-chopper winding road

*From a manuscript dated February 13, 1890, the same date Archstone Pic-
tures as the preliminary listing for this book in the Melville Log.

lonesomely skirting the pastoral uplands, a road for the most part unfenced, and in summer so little traveled that the faint wheel-tracks were traceable but on forming long, parallel depressions in the natural turf. This slant descending way the dazed one dimly recalls as joining another and less wild one leading homeward. Even so it proved. For anon he comes to the junction. There he pauses in startled recognition of a view only visible in perfection at that point ; a view deeply stamped in his memory, he having been repeatedly arrested by it when going on his hunting or birding expeditions. It was where, seen at the far end of a long vistaed clove, the head of one distant blue summit peered over the shoulder of a range not so blue as less lofty and remote. To Rip's present frame of mind, by no means normal, that summit looked like a man standing on tiptoe in a crowd to get a better look at some extraordinary object. Inquisitively it seemed to scrutinize him across the green solitudes, as much as to say—Who, I wonder, art thou ? And where, pray, didst thou come from ? This freak of his disturbed imagination was not without pain to poor Rip. That mountain, so well remembered on his part, him had it forgotten ? Quite forgotten him, and in a day ? But the evening now drawing on revives him with the sweet smells it draws from the grasses and shrubs. Proceeding on his path he, after a little, becomes sensible of a prevailing fragrance wholly new to him, at least in that vicinity, a wafted deliciousness growing more and more pronounced as he nears his house, one standing all by itself and remote from others. Suddenly, at a turn of the road, it comes into view. Hereupon, something that he misses there, and quite another thing that he sees, brings him amazed to a stand ; where, according to his hazy reminiscences, all had been without floral embellishment of any kind save a small plot of pinks and hollyhocks in the sunny rear of the house—a little garden tended by the Dame herself—lo, a lilac of unusual girth and height stands in full flower, hard by the open door, usurping, as it were, all but the very spot which he could only recall as occupied by an immemorial willow.

Now Rip's humble abode, a frame one, though indeed, as he remembered it, quite habitable, had in some particulars never been carried to entire completion; the builder and original proprietor, a certain honest woodman, while about to give it the last touches having been summoned away to join his progenitors in that paternal house where the Good Book assures us are many mansions. This sudden arrest of the work left the structure in a condition rather slatternly as to its externals. Though a safe shelter enough from the elements, ill-fitted was it as a nuptial bower for the woodman's heir, none other than Rip, his next living kin ; who, enheartened by his inheritance, boldly took the grand venture of practical life—matrimony. Yes, the first occupants were Rip and his dame, then the bride. A winsome bride it was, too, with attractiveness all her own ; her dowry consisting of little more than a chest of clothes, some cooking utensils, a bed, and a spinning wheel. A fair shape, cheeks of down, and black eyes, were hers, eyes indeed with a roguish twinkle at times, but apparently as little capable of snapping as two soft sable violets.

Well, after a few days occupying of the place, returning thereto at sunset from a romantic ramble among the low-whispering pines, Rip the while feelingly rehearsing to his beloved some memories of his indulgent mother now departed, she suddenly changed the subject. Pointing to the unfinished house, she amiably suggested to the bridegroom that he could readily do what was

needful to putting it in trim ; for was not her dear Rip a bit of a carpenter ? But Rip, rather taken at unawares, delicately pleaded something to the effect that the clattering hammer and rasping saw would be a rude disturbance to a serene charm of the honeymoon. Setting out a little orchard for future bearing would suit the time better, and this he engaged shortly to do. 'Sweetheart,' he said in conclusion, with sly magnetism, having an arm around her trim waist, 'Sweetheart, I will take up the saw and hammer in good time.' That good time proved very dilatory ; in fact, it never came. But, good or bad, time has a persistent, never-halting way of running on, and by so doing brings about wonderful changes and transformations. Ere long the bride developed into the dame ; the bridegroom into that commonplace entity, the married man. Moreover, some of those pleasing qualities which in the lover had won the inexperienced virgin's affections, turned out to be the points least desirable, as of least practical efficiency in a husband, one not born to fortune, and who therefore, to advance himself in the work-a-day world, must needs energetically elbow his way therein, quite regardless of the amenities while so doing ; either this, or else resort to the sinuous wisdom of the serpent.

Enough. Alike with the unfinished house, and its tenants new to the complexities of wedlock, things took their natural course. As to the house, never being treated to a protective coat of paint, since Rip's exchequer was always at low ebb, it soon contracted, signally upon its northern side, a gray weather-stain, supplying one topic for Dame Van Winkle's domestic reproaches ; for these in the end came, though, in the present instance, they did not wholly originate in any hard utilitarian view of matters.

Women, more than men, disrelishing the idea of old age, are sensitive, even the humblest of them, to aught in any way unpleasantly suggestive of it. And the gray weather-stain not only gave the house the aspect of age, but worse ; for in association with palpable evidences of its recentness as an erection it imparted a look forlornly human, even the look of one grown old before his time. The roof quite as much as the clapboards contributed to make noticeable in it the absence of that spirit of youth which the sex, however hard the individual lot, inheriting more of the spirit of Paradise than ourselves, would fain recognize in everything. The shingles there, with the supports for the shingle—which temporary affairs had through Rip's remissness been permanently left standing—these it took but a few autumns to veneer with thin mosses, especially in that portion where the betrayed purpose expressed by the incompleted abode had been lamented over by a huge willow—the object now missing—a willow of the weeping variety, under whose shade the house had originally been built. Broken bits of rotted twigs and a litter of discoloured leaves continually wept by this ancient Jeremiah upon the ever-greening roof of the house fatally arrested in course of completion.

No wonder that so untidy an old inhabitant had always been the object of Dame Van Winkle's dislike. And when Rip, no longer the bridegroom, in obedience to her imperative command, attacking it with an axe none the sharpest, and finding the needful energetic blows sorely jarring to the natural quiescence of his brain-pan, ignominiously gave it up, the indignant dame herself assaulted it. But the wenned trunk was of inordinate diameter, and, under the wens, of an obtuse soft toughness all but invincible to the dulled axe. In brief, the venerable old tree long remained a monument of the negative victory of stubborn inertia over spasmodic activity and an ineffectual implement.

But the scythe that advances forever and never needs whetting, sweeping that way at last, brought the veteran to the sod. Yes, during Rip's sylvan slumbers the knotty old inhabitant had been gathered to his fathers. Falling prone, and luckily away from the house, in time it made its own monument ; an ever-crumbling one, to be sure, yet, all the more for that, tenderly dressed by the Spring ; an umber-lined mound of mellow punk, mossed in spots, with wild violets springing from it here and there, attesting the place of the departed, even the same place where it fell.

But, behold ; shooting up above the low, dilapidated eaves, the lilacs now laughed where the inconsolable willow had wept. Lightly it dropped upon the green roof the pink little bells from its bunched blossoms in place of the old willow's yellowed leaves. Seen from the wood, as Rip in his reappearance viewed it, in part it furnished a gay screen to the late abode, now a tenantless ruin, hog-backed at last by the settling of the ridge-pole in the middle, abandoned to leisurely decay, and to crown the nightly rendezvous of certain disreputable ghosts, including that of Rip himself. Nevertheless, for all his sad decay and disrepute, attractiveness in these deserted premises, as the following incident may show, the interest whereof may perchance serve to justify its insertion even at this critical point.

In the month of blossoms long after Rip's disappearance in the mountain forests, followed in time by the yet more mysterious evanishment of his dame under the sod of the lowlands, a certain meditative vagabond, to wit, a young artist, in his summer wanderings among the picturesque, was so taken by the pink lilac relieved against the greenly ruinous home, that, camping under his big umbrella one fine afternoon, he opened his box of colours, brushes, and so forth, and proceeded to make a study,

While thus quietly employed he arrested the attention of a gaunt, hatchet-faced, stony-eyed individual, with a grey sort of salted complexion like that of a dried codfish, jogging by on a lank white horse. The stranger alighted, and after satisfying his curiosity as to what the artist was about, expressed his surprise that such an object as a miserable old ruin should be thought worthy painting. 'Why,' said he, 'if you must idle in this way, can find nothing useful to do, paint something respectable or better, something godly ; paint our new tabernacle—there it is,' pointing right ahead to a rectangular edifice stalk on a bare hillside, with an aspiring wooden steeple, whereon the distant blue peaks of the Kattskills looked placidly down, peradventure mildly wondering whether any rivalry with them was intended. 'Yes, paint that now,' he continued ; 'just the time for it ; it got its last coat only the other day. Ain't it white, though !'

A cadaver ! shuddered the artist to himself, glancing at it, and instantly averted his eyes. More vividly than ever he felt the difference between dead planks or dead iron smeared over with white lead ; the difference between these and white marble, when new from the quarry sparkling with the minute mica in it, or, mellowed by ages, taking on another and more genial tone endearing it to that polytheistic antiquity, the sense whereof is felt or latent in every one of us. In visionary flash he saw in their prime the perfect temples of Attica flushed with Apollo's rays on the hill-tops, or on the plain of eve disclosed in glimpses through the sacred groves around them. For the moment, in this paganish dream he quite lost himself.

'Why don't you speak ?' irritably demanded the other ; 'won't you paint it ?'

'It is sufficiently painted already, heaven knows,' said the artist, coming to himself with a discharging sigh, and now resignedly setting himself to his work.

'You will stick to this wretched old ruin, then, will you ?'

'Yes, and the lilac.'

'The lilac ? and black what-do-you-call-it— lichen, on the trunk, so old it is. It is half-rotten and its flowers spring from the rottenness under it, just as the moss from those eaves does from the rotting shingles.'

'Yes, decay is often a gardener,' asserted the other.

'What's that gibberish ? I tell you this beggarly ruin is no more a fit object for a picture than the disreputable vagabond who once lived in it.'

'Ah !' now first pricking his ears ; 'who was he ? Tell me.'

And straightway the hatchet-faced individual rehearsed, and in a sort of covertly admonitory tone, Rip's unheroic story up to the time of his mysterious disappearance. This, by the way, he imputed to a Providential visitation overtaking a lazy reprobate whose chief occupation had been to loaf up and down the country with a gun and game-box, much like others with a big umbrella and a box.

'Thank you, friend,' said the sedate one, never removing his eyes from his work ; 'Thank you ; but what should we poor devils of Bohemians do for the picturesque if Nature was in all things a precisian, each building like that church, and every man made in your image.—But bless me, what am I doing ?—I must tone down the green here.'

'Providence will take you in hand one of these days, young man,' in high dudgeon exclaimed the other. 'Yes it will give you a toning down as you call it. Made in my image ! You wrest Holy Writ ; I shake the dust off my feet and leave you.'

'Do' was the mildly acquiescent and somewhat saddish response ; and the busy brush intermitted not, while the lean visitor, remounting his lank albino, went on his way.

But presently in an elevated turn of the hill road, man and horse, outlined against the vivid blue sky, obliquely cross the Bohemian's sight, and the next moment, as if swallowed up by the grave, disappeared in the descent.

'What is that verse in the Apocalypse' murmured the artist to himself, now suspending the brush and ruminatingly turning his head sideways, 'the verse that prompted Benjamin West to his big canvas ?—"And I looked and beheld a pale horse, and his name that sat on him was Death."—Well, I won't allegorise and be mystical, and all that, nor even say that Death dwells not under the cemetery turf, since rather it is Sleep inhabits thee ; no, only this much will I say, that to-day have I seen him, even Death, seen him in the guise of a living man on a living horse ; that he dismounted and had speech with me ; and that, though an unpleasant sort of person, and even a queer threatener withal, yet, if one meets him, one must get along with him as one can ; for his ignorance is extreme. And what under heaven indeed should such a phantasm as Death know, for all that the appearance tacitly claims to be somebody that knows much ?'

Luck is a good deal in this world. Had the Bohemian, instead of chancing that way when he did,

come into the same season but a few years later, the
period of the present recital, who knows but that the
opportunity might have been furnished him of sketching
tattered Rip himself in his picturesque resurrection,
bewildered, and at a stand before his own door, even as
erewhile we left him.

Ere sighting the premises, Rip's doddering
faculties had been sufficiently nonplussed by various
unaccountable appearances such as branch roads which
he could not recall, and fields rustling with young grain
where he seemed to remember waving woods ; so that
now the absence of the old willow and its replacement
by the lilac—a perfect stranger, standing sentry at his
own door, as it were, challenging his right to further
approach—these phenomena quite confounded him.

Recovering his senses a little, while yet with
one hand against his wrinkled brow, remaining bodily
transfixed, in wondering sort half unconsciously he
begins :—

'Ay,—no !—my brain is addled yet ;
With last night's flagons-full I forget.
But look !—well, well, it so must be,
For there it is, and, sure, I see.
Yon lilac is all right, no doubt,
Though never before, Rip—spied him out !
But where is the willow ?—dear, dear me !
This is the hill-side, sure ;—the stream
Flows yon ; and that, wife's house would seem
But for the silence. Well, maybe,
For this one time—ha ! do I see
Those burdocks going in at door ?
They only loitered round before !
No,—ay !—bless me, it is the same !
But yonder lilac ! how now came—

Rip, where does Rip Van Winkle live?
Lilac ?—a lilac ? Why, just there,
If my cracked memory don't deceive,
'Twas I set out a lilac fair,
Yesterday morning, seems to me.
Yea, sure, that it might thrive and come
To plead for me with wife, though dumb.
I found it—dear me—well, well, well,
Squirrels and angels, they can tell !
My head !—whose head ?— Ah, Rip (I'm Rip),
That lilac was a little slip,
And yonder lilac is a tree !'

But why rehearse in every section
The withered good-fellow's resurrection,
Happily told by happiest Irving
Never from genial verity swerving ;
And, more to make the story rife,
By Jefferson acted thus to life.
Me here it behooves to tell
Of things that posthumously fell.

It came to pass as years went on
(An Indian file in stealthy flight
With purpose never man has known)
A villa brave transformed the sight
Of Rip's abode to nothing gone,
Himself remanded into night.
Each time the owner joyance found
In one prized tree that held its ground,
One tenant old where all was new,—
Rip's lilac to its youth still true.
Despite its slant ungainly trunk,
Atwist and black like strands in junk,

Annual yet it flowered aloft
In juvenile pink complexion soft.

That owner hale, long past his May,
His children's children—every one
Like those Rip romped with in the sun—
Merrily plucked the clusters gay.
The place a stranger scented out
By Boniface told in vinous way—
'Follow the fragrance !' Truth to own,
Such reaching wafture ne'er was blown
From common Lilac. Came about
That neighbours, unconcerned before
When bloomed the tree by lowly door,
Craved now one little slip to train ;
Neighbour from neighbour begged again.
On every hand stem shot from slip,
Till, lo, that region now is dowered
Like the first Paradise embowered,
Thanks to poor good-for-nothing Rip !

Some think those parts should bear his name ;
But no—the blossoms take the fame.
Slant finger-posts by horsemen scanned
Point the green miles—*to Lilac Land.*

Go ride there down one charmful lane,
O reader mine, when June's at best,
A dream of Rip shall slack the rein,
For there his heart flowers out confessed.
And there you'll say—O, hard ones, truce !
See, where man finds in man no ruse,
Boon Nature finds one—Heaven be blest !

PART IV—AS THEY TELL

A ROSE OR TWO

A GROUND VINE

INTERCEDES WITH THE QUEEN OF FLOWERS FOR THE
MERITED RECOGNITION OF CLOVER

Hymned down the years from ages far,
The theme of lover, seer, and king,
Reign endless, Rose ! for fair you are,
Nor heaven reserves a fairer thing.
To elfin ears the bell-flowers chime
Your beauty, Queen, your fame ;
Your titles, blown thro' Ariel's clime,
Thronged trumpet-flowers proclaim.

Not less with me, a groundling bear,
Here bold for once, by nature shy ;—
If votaries yours be everywhere,
And flattering you the laureates vie—
Meekness the more your heart should share.

O Rose, we plants are all akin,
Our roots enlock ; each strives to win
The ampler space, the sunnier air.
But beauty, plainness, shade and sun—
Here share-and-share-alike is none !

And ranked with grass, a flower may dwell,
Cheerful, if never high in feather,
With pastoral sisters thriving well
In bloom that shares the harder weather,
Charmful, mayhap, in simple grace,
A lowlier Eden mantling in her face,

My Queen, so all along I lie,
But creep I can, scarce win your eye.
But O, your garden-wall peer over,
And, if you blush, 'twill hardly be
At owning kin with Cousin Clover
Who winsome makes the low degree.

THE AVATAR

Bloom of repute for graft or seed
In flowers the flower-gods never heed,
The Rose-God once came down and took
Form in a rose ? Nay, but indeed
The meeker form and humbler look
Of Sweet-Briar, a wilding weed.

ROSARY BEADS

I.
THE ACCEPTED TIME

Adore the Roses ; nor delay
Until the rose-fane fall,
Or ever their censers cease to sway :
'To-day !' the rose-priests call.

II.
WITHOUT PRICE

Have the Roses. Needs no pelf
The blooms to buy,
Nor any rose-bed to thyself
Thy skill to try :
But live up to the Rose's light,
Thy meat shall turn to roses red,
Thy bread to roses white.

III.
GRAIN BY GRAIN

Grain by grain the Desert drifts
Against the Garden-Land :
Hedge well thy Roses, heed the stealth
Of ever-creeping Land.

HEARTH-ROSES

The Sugar-Maple embers in bed
Here fended in Garden of Fire,
Like the Roses yield musk,
Like the Roses are Red,
Like the Roses expire
Lamented when low ;
But excelling the flower,
Are odorous in ashes
As e'en in their glow.

Ah, Love, when life closes,
Dying the death of the just,
May we vie with Hearth-Roses,
Smelling sweet in our dust.

THE NEW ROSICRUCIANS

To us, disciples of the Order
Whose Rose-Vine twines the Cross,
Who have drained the rose's chalice
Never heeding gain or loss ;
For all the preacher's din
There is no mortal sin—
No, none to us but Malice.

Exempt from that, in blest recline
We let life's billows toss ;
If sorrow come, anew we twine
The Rose-Vine round the Cross.

THE VIAL OF ATTAR

Lesbia's lover when bereaved
In pagan times of yore
Ere the gladsome tidings ran
Of reunion evermore,
He wended from the pyre
Now hopeless in return—
Ah, the vial hot with tears
For the ashes cold in urn !

But I, the Rose's lover,
When *my* beloved goes
Followed by the Asters
Toward the sepulchre of snows,
Then, solaced by the vial

Less grieve I for the Tomb,
Not widowed of the fragrance
If parted from the bloom.
Parted from the bloom
That was lost for a day ;
Rose ! I dally with thy doom !
The solace will not stay !
There is nothing like the bloom ;
And the Attar poignant minds me
Of the bloom that's passed away.

UNDER THE SNOW
THE AMBUSCADE

Meek crossing of the bosom's lawn
Averted scenery veil-like drawn,
Well beseem thee, nor obtrude
The cloister of thy virginhood,
And yet, white ruin, that seemly dress
Of purity pale passionless,
A May-snow is ; for fleeting term,
Custodian of love's lumbering germ—
Nay, nurtures it, till time disclose
Now frost-fed Amor's burning rose.

IN SHARDS THE SYLVAN VASES LIE

In shards the sylvan vases lie,
Their links of dance undone ;
And brambles wither by thy brim,
Choked Fountain of the Sun !
The spider in the laurel spins,
The weed exiles the flower,
And, flung to kiln, Apollo's bust
Makes lime for Mammon's tower.

AMOROSO

Rosamond, my Rosamond
Of roses is the rose ;
Her bloom belongs to summer
Nor less in winter glows,
When, mossed in furs all cosy,
We speed it o'er the snows
By ice-bound streams enchanted,
While red Arcturus, he
A huntsman ever ruddy
Sees a ruddier star by me.

O Rosamond, Rose Rosamond,
Is yonder Dian's reign ?
Look, the icicles despond
Chill drooping from her fane !
But Rosamond, Rose Rosamond,
In us, a plighted pair,
First makes with flame a bond—
One purity they share.
To feel your cheek like ice,
While snug the furs enclose—
This is spousal love's device
This is Arctic Paradise,
And wooing in the snows !
Rosamond, my Rosamond,
Rose Rosamond, Moss-Rose !

UNDER THE SNOW

Between a garden and old tomb
Disused, a foot-path threads the clover ;

And there I met the gardener's boy
Bearing some dewy chaplets over.

I marveled, for I just had passed
The charnel vault and shunned its gloom :
' Stay, whither wend you, laden thus ;
Roses ! you would not these inhume ? '

' Yea, for against the bridal hour
My master fain would keep their bloom ;
A charm in the dank o' the vault there is,
Yea we the rose entomb.'

THE ROSE WINDOW

The preacher took from Solomon's Song
Four words for text with mystery rife—
The Rose of Sharon, figuring Him
The Resurrection and the Life ;
And, pointing many an urn in new
How honeyed a homily he drew.

There in the slumberous afternoon,
Through minster grey, in lullaby rolled
The brimmed metheglin charged with swoon
Drowsy, my decorous hands I fold
Till sleep overtakes with dream for boon.

I saw an Angel with a Rose
Come out of Morning's garden-gate,
And lamp-like hold the Rose aloft ;
He entered a sepulchral Strait,
I followed. And I saw the Rose
Shed dappled down upon the dead ;

The shrouds and mort-cloths all were lit
To plaids and chequered tartans red.

I woke, the great Rose-Window high,
A mullioned wheel in gable set,
Suffused with rich and soft in dye
Where Iris and Amora met ;
Aslant in sheaf of rays it threw
From all its foliate round of panes
Transfiguring light on dingy stains,
While danced the motes in dusty pew.

THE DEVOTION OF THE FLOWERS
TO THEIR LADY

Attributed to Clement Dronon, a monk, a Provençal of noble birth
in the eleventh century, in earlier life a troubadour, a devotee of
Love and the Rose, but eventually, like some others of his stamp in
that age, for an unrevealed cause retiring from the gay circles where
he had long been a caressed favourite, and ultimately disappearing
from the world in a monastery.

TO OUR QUEEN

O Queen, we are loyal : shall sad ones forget ?
We are natives of Eden—
Sharing its memory with you,
And your handmaidens yet.

You bravely dissemble with looks that beguile
Musing mortals to murmur
Reproachful 'So festal, O Flower,
We but weary the while ?

What, nothing has happened ? No event to make wan,
Begetting things hateful—

Old age, decay, and the sorrows,
Devourers of man ?'

They marvel and marvel how come you so bright,
When the splendour, the joyance—
Florid revel of joyance
The Cypress in sight !

Scarce *you* would poor Adam, upbraid that his fall
Like a landslide by waters
Rolled an outspreading impulse
Disordering all ;

That the Angel indignant, with eyes that foreran
The betrayed generations,
Cast out the flowers wherewith Eve
Decked her nuptials with man.

Ah, exile is exile tho' spiced by the sod,
In Shushan we languish—
Languish with the secret desire
For the garden of God.

But all of us yet
We the Lilies whose pallor is passion,
We the Pansies that muse nor forget
In harbinger airs how we freshen,
When, clad in the amice of gray silver-hemmed
Meek coming in twilight and dew,
The Day-Spring, with pale, priestly hand and
        begemmed,
Touches and coronates you :—

Breathing, O daughter of far descent,
Banished, yet blessed in banishment,
Whereto is appointed a term ;
Flower, voucher of Paradise, visible pledge,
Rose, attesting it spite of the Worm.

THY AIM, THY AIM ?

Thy aim, thy aim?
'Mid the dust dearth, and din,
An exception wouldst win
By some deed shall ignite the acclaim ?
Then beware, and prepare thee
Lest Envy ensnare thee
And yearning be sequelled by shame.
But strive bravely on, yet on, and yet on,
Let the goal be won ;
Then if, living, you kindle a flame,
Your guerdon will be but a flower,
Only a flower,
The flower of repute,
A flower cut down in an hour.
But repute, if this be too tame,
And, dying, you truly ennoble a name—
Again but a flower !
Only a flower,
A funeral flower,
A blossom of Dis from Proserpine's bower—
The belated funeral flower of fame.

PART V—THE ROSE FARMER

THE ROSE FARMER

Coming through the rye ;
Thereof the rural poet whistles ;
But who the flute will try
At scrambling through the thistles !
Nor less upon some roseate way
Emerge the prickly passage may.

But we who after ragged scrambles
Through fate's blessed thorns and brambles
Come unto our roses late—
Aright to manage the estate,
This indeed it well may task us,
Quite inexperienced as we be
In aught but thickets that unmasque us
Of man's ennobling drapery.

Indigence in a plain estate :
Riches imply the complicate.
What peevish, pestering wants surprise,
What bothering ambitions rise !
Then, too, Fate loans a lot luxurious
At such hard cent-per-cent usurious !
Mammon, never meek as Moses,
Gouty, mattressed on moss-roses,
A crumpled rose-leaf makes him furious.
Allow, as one's purveyor here
Of sweet content, of Christian cheer,

'Vile Pelf,' we overestimate.
Howbeit, a rose-farm nigh Damascus
Would Dives change at even rate
Lazarus' snow-farm in Alaskas ?

But that recalls me : I return.—
A friend, whose shadow has decreased,
For whom they reared a turbaned urn,
A corpulent grandee of the East,
Whose kind goodwill to me began
When I against his Ramadan
Prepared a chowder for his feast,
Well dying, he remembered me ;
A brave bequest, a farm in fee
Forever consecrate to roses,
And laved by streams that sacred are,
Pharpar in twin-born Abana,
Which last the pleasure-ground encloses,
At least winds half-way round about—
That garden to caress, no doubt.

But, ah, the stewardship it poses !
Every hour the bloom, the bliss
Upbraid me that I am remiss,
For still I dally—I delay—
Long do hesitate, and say,
'Of fifty thousand Damask Roses—
(For my rose-farm no great matter)
Shall I make me heaps of posies,
Or some few crystal drops of Attar ?
To smell or sell, or for a boon'.

Quick you cull a rose and easy ;
But Attar is not got so soon,
Demanding more than gesture breezy.

Yet this same Attar, I suppose,
Long time will last, outlive indeed,
The rightful sceptre of the rose
And coronations of the weed.

Sauntering, plunged in this debate,
And somewhat leaning to elect
The thing most easy to effect,
I chanced upon a Persian late,
A sort of gentleman-rose-farmer
On knees beside his garden-gate
Telling his beads, just like a palmer.
Beads ? Coins, I meant. Each golden one
Upon a wire of silver run ;
And every time a coin he told
His brow he raised, and eyes he rolled
Devout in grateful orison.

Surely, methought, this pious man,
A florist, too, will solve my doubt.
Saluting him, I straight began :
'Decide, I pray, a dubious matter—'
And put the roses and the Attar.
Whereat the roses near and far—
For all his garden was a lawn
Of roses thick as daisies are
In meads from smoky towns withdrawn—

They turned their heads like ladies when
They hear themselves discussed by men.
But he, he swerved a wrinkled face,
Elderly, yet with ruddy trace—
Tinged doubly by warm flushings thrown
From sunset's roses and his own ;

And, after scanning me and sounding,
'And you ?—an older man than I ?
Late come you with your sage propounding :
Allah ! your time has long gone by.'—
'Indeed, sir, but so ruled the fate
I came unto my roses late.
When then ? These gray hairs but disguise,
Since down in heart youth never dies—
O sharpened by the long delay,
I'm eager for my roses quite ;
But first would settle this prime matter—
Touching the roses and the Attar :
I fear to err there ; set me right.'

Meseemed his purs'd eyes grateful twinkled
Hearing of veteran youth unwrinkled,
Himself being old. But now the answer
Direct came like a changing lancer :
'Attar ? Go ask the Parsee yonder.
Lean as a rake with his distilling,
Cancel his debts, scarce worth a shilling !
How he exists I frequent wonder.
No neighbour loves him : sweet endeavour
Will get a nosegay from him never ;
No, nor even your ducats will ;
A very save-all for his still !
Of me, however, all speak well :
You see my little coins I tell ;
I give away, but more I sell,
In mossy pots or bound in posies,
Always a market for my roses.
But Attar, why, it comes so dear
'Tis far from popular, that's clear.
I flourish, I ; yon heavens they bless me,
My darlings cluster to caress me.'

At that fond sentence overheard,
Methought his rose seraglio stirred.
But further he : 'Yon Parsee lours
Headsman and Blue Beard of the flowers.
In virgin flushed with efflorescence
When buds their bosoms just disclose,
To get a mummified quintessence
He scimetars the living rose !
I grant, against my different way,
Something, and specious, one might say,
Ay, pluck a rose in dew Auroral,
For buttonette to please the sight—
The dawn's bloom and the bloom but floral,
Why, what a race with them in flight !
Quick, too, the redolence it stales.
And yet you have the brief delight,
And yet the next morn's bud avails ;
And on in sequence.' Came that close,
And, lo, in each flushed garden bed,
What agitation ! Every rose
Bridling aloft the passionate head !
But what it was that angered here—
Just why the high resentment shown,
Pray ask of her who'll hint it clear—
A Mormon's first wife making moan.

But he, rose-farmer, long time versed
In roses husbanded by him,
Letting a glance upon them skim,
Followed his thread and more rehearsed ;
And, waxing now a trifle warm :
'This evanescence is the charm !
And most it wins the spirits that be
Celestial, sir. It comes to me

It was this fleeting charm in show
That lured the sons of God below,
Tired out with perpetuity
Of heaven's own seventh heaven aglow ;
Not Eve's fair daughters, sir ; nay, nay,
Less fugitive in charm are they :
It was the rose.' As this he said
So flattering in imputation,—
Angelic sweethearts overheard,
Even seraphs paying them adoration ;
Each rose, as favouring the whim
Grave nodded,—as attesting him.

'But now, sir, for your urgent matter.
Every way—for wise employment,
Repute and profit, health, enjoyment,
I am for roses—sink the Attar !'

And hereupon the downright man
To tell his rosary re-began.
And never a rose in all the garden
Blushed deeper there to hear their warden
So forcefully express his mind.
Methought they even seemed to laugh—
True ladies who, in temper kind,
Will pardon aught, though unrefined,
Sincerely vouched in their behalf.

Discreet, in second thought's immersion
I wended from this prosperous Persian
Who, verily, seemed in life rewarded
For sapient prudence not amiss,
Nor transcendental essence hoarded
In hope of quintessential bliss :

No, never with painstaking throes
Essays to crystallize the rose.
But here arrest the loom—the line.
Though Damask be your precious stuff,
Spin it not out too superfine :
The flower of a subject is enough.

L'ENVOI

Rosy dawns the morning Syrian,
       Youthful as in years of Noah ;
       Why then aging at three-score ?
Do moths infest your mantle Tyrian ?
       Shake it out where the sunbeams pour !
Time, amigo, does not masque us—
       Boys in gray wigs, young at core.
Look, what demigods of Damascus,
       Roses, lure to Pharpar's shore !
Sigh not—Age, dull tranquilliser,
       And arid years that filed before,
For flowers unfit us. Nay, be wiser :
       Wiser in relish, if sedate,
Come graybeards to their roses late.

ADDITIONAL POEMS

IRIS
(1865/1874)

When Sherman's march was over,
   And June was green and bright,
She came among out mountains,
   A freak of new delight ;
Provokingly our banner
   Salutes with Dixie's strain—
Little rebel from Savannah,
   Three Colonels in her train.

Three bearded Puritan colonels :
   But oh, her eyes, her mouth—
Magnolias in their langour,
   And sorcery of the South.
High-handed rule of beauty,
   Are wars for man but vain ?
Behold, three disenslavers,
   Themselves embrace a chain !

But, loveliest invader,
   Out of Dixie did ye rove,
By sallies of your raillery
   To rally us, or move ?
For under all your merriment
   There lurked a minor tone ;

And of havoc we had tidings
      And a roof-tree overthrown.

Ah, nurtured in the trial
      And ripened by the storm,
Was your gaiety your courage
      And levity its form ?
O'er your future's darkling waters,
      O'er your past, a frozen tide,
Like the petrel would you skim it,
      Like the glancing skaters glide ?

But the ravisher has won her
      Who the wooers three did slight ;
To his fastness he has borne her
      By the trail that leads through night.
With peace she came, the rainbow,
      And like a bow did pass,
The balsam trees exhaling,
      And tear-drops in the grass.

Now laughed the leafage over
      Her pranks in woodland scene :
Hath left for us the revel
      Deep in paradise the green ?
In truth we will believe it
      Under pines that sigh a balm,
Though o'er thy stone be trailing
      Cypress-moss that drapes the palm.

1

Madam Mirror

— ·· —

With wrecks in a garret I'm stranded,
Whae, no longer returning a face,
I take to reflections the deeper
On memories far to retrace.

In me have all people confided,
The maiden her charms has displayed
And truths unrevealed and unuttered
To me have been freely betrayed.

MADAM MIRROR

With wrecks in a garret I'm stranded,
Where, no longer returning a face,
I take to reflections the deeper
On memories far to retrace.

In me have all people confided,
The maiden her charms has displayed,
And truths unrevealed and unuttered
To me have been freely betrayed.

Some truths I might tell of the toilet,
Did not tenderness make me forget ;
But the glance of proud beauty slow fading,
It dies not away from me yet ;
Not the eyes too long ceasing to shine—
Soliciting, shunning, well knowing that mine
Were too candid to flatter when met.

But pledged unto trueness forever,
My confessional close as the friar's,
How sacred to me are the trusting,
Here nothing for scandal transpires.

But ah, what of all this is perished,
Nor less shall again be, again !
What pangs after parties of pleasure,
What smiles but disclosures of pain !

O, the tears of the hopeless unloved,
O, start at old age drawing near—
And what shadows of thoughts more tragical far
Like clouds on a lake have been here !

Tho' lone in a loft I must languish,
Far from closet and parlour at strife,
Content I escape from the anguish
Of the Real and the Seeming in life.

THE WISE VIRGINS
TO MADAM MIRROR

Madam Mirror, believe we are sorry for you ;
But ah, how console you or cheer !
We are young, we go skipping, but you
Are an old and forlorn garreteer !
'Tis we view the world thro' an arbour,
The bride with the bridegroom appears ;
But you, retrospecting thro' tunnels,
See but widowers and widows on biers !
To us that is foreign, in no sense will pair
With cake, wine and diamonds, and blossoms in hair !

But age !—ah, the crow will scarce venture
To tread near the eyes flashing bold ;
He 's a craven ; and youth is immortal ;
'Tis the elderly only grow old !

But, Dame, for all misty recurrings
To beacons befogged in the past—
Less dismal they are, Dame, than dubious ;
Nor joy leaves us time to forecast.

Tho' the battered we hardly would banter,
And never will ridicule use,
Let us say that a twilight of inklings
Is worth scarce the Pope's old shoes.

For the rest, the skeletons meeting glass eyes
Let a parable serve, if by chance it applies.
A brace of green goggles they gabbled, old elves,
Touching my queer spectacles they had descried ;
But the queerest of all were the goggles themselves,
Rusty, fusty shagreen of the puckered fish-hide !
But you, Madam Mirror, not here we type you,
Nor twit you for being a glass
With a druggish green blur and a horrible way
Of distorting all objects, alas !

Ourselves, so symmetric, our cavaliers tell,
What, squint us to witches with broomsticks to sell !
Oh yes, we are giddy, we whirl in youth's waltz,
But a fig for Reflections when crookedly false !

IMMOLATED

Children of my happier prime,
When One yet lived with me, and threw
Her rainbow over life and time,
Even Hope, my bride, and mother to you !
O, nurtured in sweet pastoral air,
And fed on flowers and light and dew
Of morning meadows—spare, ah, spare
Reproach ; spare, and upbraid me not
That, yielding scarce to reckless mood,
But jealous of your future lot,
I sealed you in a fate subdued.
Have I not saved you from the drear
Theft, and ignoring which need be
The triumph of the insincere
Unanimous Mediocrity ?
Rest therefore, free from all despite,
Snugged in the arms of comfortable night.

SHADOW AT THE FEAST
MRS. B_____

(1847)

Now churches are leafy,
Now evergreens reign ;
'Tis green Birnam wood
Come to gray Dunsinane !

Now the night it is starry,
And lavishly go,
In a largess of music,
The bells thro' the snow.

Now burn the decanters
Like turrets that rise,
All garnet in sunset
Of orient skies.

O, snugged in the Valley,
A homestead of hearts !
Love flies like a shuttle,
And knits while it darts.

Brown brothers, fair sisters,
Bright cousins and all,
Keeping Christmas at table,
The large and the small.

But a kinswoman glideth,
Infantile in grace,
Sits down and is silent—
Medallion in place !

O, the hearth is like ruby,
The curtains they glow ;
But she who sits sadly
Her story we know :

The blossom of orange'
Turned cypress so soon !
Child-bride of the May-time,
Child-widow in June !

Snow-white is her raiment ;
And sorrow so mild,
An elf-sorrow seemeth,
As she an elf-child.

In patience she sitteth ;
Though cometh no balm,
She floats, holy lily,
On waters of calm.

Come, pass the decanter !
Our hearts let us cheer,
Yea, I wish *Merry Christmas*—
But let her not hear !

The Old Boy of the Cave.

(See Lyell's Antiquity of man)
and Falmouth's ... of ...

— 11 —

The man of bone confirms this theme
  In cave where fossils be;
Outdating every mummy known,
Not older Cuvier's mastodon,
  Nor older much the sea:
Old as the Glacial Period, he;
And claims he calls to mind the day
When Thule's king, by reindeer drawn,
His sleigh-bells jingling in icy morn,
Slid clean from the Pole to the Wetterhorn
Over frozen waters in May!
      Oh the man of the cave of Engihoul,
      With Eld doth he dote and drule?

THE NEW ANCIENT OF DAYS
THE MAN OF THE CAVE OF ENGIHOUL

(See Lyell's *The Antiquity of Man*
and Darwin's *The Descent of the Species.*)

The man of bone confirms his throne
    In cave where fossils be ;
Out-dating every mummy known,
Not older Cuvier's mastodon,
    Nor older much the sea :
    Old as Glacial Period, he ;
And claims he calls to mind the day
When Thule's king, by reindeer drawn,
His sleigh-bells jingling in icy morn,
Slid clean from the Pole to the Wetterhorn
Over frozen waters in May !
      O, the man of the cave in Engihoul,
      With Eld doth he dote and drule ?

A wizard one, his lore is none
    Ye spell with A, B, C :
But dodo tracks, all up and down
That slate he poreth much upon,
    This algebra may be :—
    Yea, there he ciphers and sums it free ;
To ages ere Indus met ocean's swell
Addeth aeons ere Satan or Saturn fell.
His totals of time make an awful schism,
And old Chronos he pitches adown the abysm
Like a pebble down Carisbrooke well.
      Yea, the man of the cave of Engihoul
      from Moses knocks under the stool.

In bas-relief he late has shown
    A terrible show, agree—
Megalosaurus, iguanadon,

Palaeotherium, glyphthaecon,
      A Barnum's show raree ;
      The vomit of slimy and sludgy sea ;
Purposeless creatures, odd inchoate things
Which splashed thro' morasses on fleshly wings ;
The cubs of Chaos, with eyes askance,
Preposterous griffins that squint at Chance
And Anarch's crazed decree !
      O, the showman who dens in Engihoul,
      Would he fright us, or quit us, or fool ?

But needs to own, he takes a tone,
      Satiric on nobs, pardee !
'Though in ages whose term is yet to run,
Old Adam a seraph may have for son,
      His gran'ther's a crab, d'ye see !
      And why cut your kinsman the ape ?' adds he :
'Your trick of scratching is borrowed from him,
Grimace and cunning with many a whim,
Your fidgets and hypoes, and each megrim—
All's traced in the family tree !'
      Ha, the wag of the cave of Engihoul :
      Buss me, gorilla and ghoul !

Obstreperous grown he'd fain dethrone
      Joe Smith and e'en Jones Three ;
Against even Jos and great Mahone
He flings his fossilipher's stone
      And rattles his shanks for glee.
      I'll settle these parvenu fellows, he-he !
Diluvian Ore of Ducaliaon's day—
A parting take to the Phocene clay.
He swears no Ens that take a name
Commensurate is with the vasty claim
Of the protoplastic Fegee.
      O, the spook of the cave of Engihoul
      He flogs us and sends us to school.

Hyena of bone! Ah, beat him down,
    Great Pope, with Peter's key,
Ere the Grand Pan-Jam be overthrown
With Joe and Jos and great Mahone,
    And the firmament mix with the sea ;
    And then, my masters, where should we be ?
But the ogre of bone he snickers alone,
And grins for his godless glee.
'I have flung my stone, my fossil stone,
And your gods, they scamper," saith he.
    Imp ! Imp of the cave of Engihoul
    Shall he grin like the Gorgon and rule ?

HONOUR

With jeweled tusks and damask housings,
August the elephants appear :
Grandees, trumpets, banners, soldiers—
One flame from van to rear !

Bid by India's King they travel
In solemn embassage to-day,
To meet the Diamond from Golconda,
The Great Find of Cathay.

O the honour, O the homage !
But, methinks, 'twere nice,
Would they say but *How-de-do* ?
To the Little Pearl of Price.

After Herman's death in 1891 Lizzie Shaw Melville moved from their East 26th Street house to an apartment eight blocks south, filling her library with Melville's collection of books. In one of them Lizzie marked the following passage by Isaac Disraeli's widow. It clearly had personal resonance for her.

> *"My ideas of my husband . . . are so much associated with his books, that to part with them would be as it were breaking some of the last ties which still connect me with so beloved an object. The being in the midst of books he has been accustomed to read, and which contain his marks and notes, will still give him a sort of existence with me."*

From Andrew Delbanco's *Melville His World and Work*, 2005

HERMAN MELVILLE: Biographical Notes
August 1, 1819 – September 28, 1891

For years I have listened to people protest the scholastic requirement of reading Herman Melville's novel, *Moby-Dick*. The complaints are legitimate but the truth behind the trouble with the book is not really justified. As the author of five previous novels (*Typee: A Peep at Polynesian Life*, 1946; *Omoo: A Narrative of Adventure in the South Seas*, 1846; *Mardi: and a Voyage Thither*, 1849; *Redburn: His First Voyage*, 1849; *White-Jacket: or The World in a Man-Of-War*, 1850) the author broke new ground in his fiction with his 1851 book.

All of his work had been based on true stories; some he lived, some he heard about or read about. His fiction was historical fiction in the best sense of that genre. His first two books were very successful, establishing him as a writer of exciting, true-to-life tales that young men could read with pleasure. His next three were less successful and with *Moby-Dick* he broke new ground by harking back to a fiction format that had been best exemplified by Miguel de Cervantes' two-volume novel, *The Ingenious Gentleman Don Quixote of La Mancha*, written in 1605 and 1615. Both works are episodic books written in the picaresque style (although Cervantes' work is truly humorous and Melville's is not except for incidental passages that truly delight). Each novel tells a straightforward narrative tale interspersed with history lessons, cultural insights, examinations of legends and myths, culinary lessons, stories from other countries and other peoples, all of which have nothing to do with the main story. Melville's research for these inserted interruptions are principally what have made *Moby-Dick* a challenge to modern readers just as they were for readers in his own time.

In his third novel, Mardi, he inserted seven poems he had written and these did not help that book with a public that had not conceived of Melville as a poet. "A ray of the moon on the dancing waves / Is the step, light step of that beautiful maid: / Mardi, with music, her footfall paves, / And her voice, no voice, but a song in the glade." [Mardi; Chapter 132] Poetry, it seems, had entered his world early. By 1859 with the national struggle for unity and peace collapsing he began to write poetry with a serious intent. With *The Portent*, written in 1859 and using seaman's terminology [Hanging from the beam, / slowly swaying (such is the law)] and *Misgivings*, written in 1860 [When ocean-clouds over inland hills / Sweet storming in late Autumn brown, / And horror the sodden valley fills, / And the spire falls crashing in the town,] he predicts the coming Civil War.

The critical and popular failure of *Moby-Dick* greatly affected Melville's output in the years that followed at Arrowhead, his home in The Berkshires. He wrote three more novels (*Pierre: or The Ambiguities*, 1852; *Israel Potter: His fifty Years of Exile,*1855; *The Confidence-Man*, 1857) and a group of shorter fiction that included *Bartleby, the Scrivener*, 1853, *The Encentadas*, 1854, *Benito Cereno*, 1855, *I and My Chimney*, 1856 and at least thirteen more, all of which enjoyed a degree of success. However, after the failure of his last novel in 1857 he turned more and more to his poetry.

He published four books of poetry: *Battle-Pieces and Aspects of the War* in 1866, *Clarel, a Poem and Pilgrimage in the Holy Land* in 1876, *John Marr and Other Sailors* (which included his first mention of *Billy Budd, Sailor*) in 1888, and *Timoleon* in 1891, the year he died. At the time of his death in September of that year he had also completed a version of *Weeds and Wildings, chiefly; With a Rose or Two*, his last collection of poetry and short fiction, dedicated to his wife. In spite of all this output he was literally a forgotten man at the time of his death. The *New York Times* obituary cited only one work in its farewell, *Typee*. The *Pittsfield Sun* credited him with that book and with *Omoo*. One obituary referred to him as Henry Melville, so far forgotten by the public that even his name escaped that particular author.

American poet and literary critic Randall Jarrell whose work for the magazine, *The New Republic*, under the watchful eye of Editor Edmund Wilson, helped to foster the careers of poets William Carlos Williams, Elizabeth Bishop and Robert Lowell, wrote that he ranked Walt Whitman, Emily Dickinson and Herman Melville as America's best 19th century poets. Perhaps it was Jarrell's own poetry about the second world war that put him in sync with Melville and Whitman, both of whom wrote extensively on the Civil War.

What makes the poetry in this volume so very compelling is the im-mediacy of the work; each poem talks to us of an instant in time, a perfect picture of what it meant to be there, to experience through his senses what he recalled so poetically. Melville's journey through the years, back to Arrowhead in Pittsfield, Massachusetts where he had spent so many productive periods, touches our own memories and our senses with language that begs to be read aloud. Reading the chapters in *Moby-Dick* that are not a part of the basic narrative of Ahab, Ishmael, the whale and so on, out loud makes them more than just tolerable. The music in Melville's language, the poetry that infuses his writing, makes those sections into richly rewarding adventures of their own.

Similarly, reading the poems in this book out loud gives them weight, gravity, emotional support and allows us insights into the mind of a genius who, before his time, invented worlds that would make our contemporary world so much richer. Like the poet Edna St. Vincent Millay, half a century later, Melville's work feels new and a part of our own time even when the picture he draws is a bit arcane, secret and private and known only to its creator. His precious world is accessible and beautiful and stirring when you give to it what the author himself gave it: a voice.

J. Peter Bergman
Director of Communications and CommunityRelations

GLOSSARY OF UNUSUAL WORDS AND REFERENCES

Abana: a river that crosses the plains of Damascus

Amice: a liturgical garment, a collar worn under the alb

Ceres: an asteroid discovered in 1801 whose orbit is between Mars and
      Jupiter

Chaplet: a garland or wreath to be worn on the head

Coppice: a thicket, or grove

Dibbling: making holes in the soil

Dives: disreputable resorts for drinking and entertainment

Engihoul: cave on the western side of the Meuse river where human
      remains were discovered in the 1830s challenging known
      theories about the origins of man.

Fane: weathercock

Golconda: a fortresss in the Hyderabad district of India, a region that
      has produced the Hope diamond, the Nassak diamond and the
      Kohi-Noor

Jefferson: in the Rip Van Winkle poem the reference is to the American
      actor Joseph Jefferson (1829-1905) who played Rip from 1859
      until his death; the Chicago theatre awards are named for him.

Mattock: an implement combining aspects of an axe and a pick

Metheglin: medicated beverage made with mulled honey

Minster: monastery or churchyard

Pelf: property or belongings

Pharpar: a biblical river in Syria, sister to the Abana river

Poignard: a slight dagger with a triangular or square blade

Prank: to adorn in a gay or merry manner

Ruddock: a robin

Saccharine: relating to the nature of sugar fermenting

Shushan: biblical palace where Daniel saw one of his visions and where
      most of the story of Esther takes place

Sward: a portion of ground covered with grass, turf, sod

Tares: seeds of the vetch

Tipple: squander

Tyrian: from ancient Tyre, a Phoenician city, the special hue of purple

Ver: the season of spring

Votaries: ardent enthusiasts

Welkin: the vault of Heaven; the firmament, the sky.

Wight: preternatural being such as a fairy or a witch

Winnow: separate and drive off

Chimney Room at Arrowhead, circa 1870

ARROWHEAD

Purchased from Dr. John Brewster on September 14, 1850 by Herman Melville, the house had a history of its own by that time. For $6500 he acquired "a large quaint old house" and 160 acres of land. It was the same price the Morewood family had paid for the 255 acre plot of land adjacent to Melville's that had been his Uncle's farm (now the Pittsfield Country Club on route 7/20), the home he himself had hoped to buy. The new house was just down the road from the Oliver Wendell Holmes farm, overlooked the Housatonic River and had open, unobstructed views north to Mount Greylock. The property included open fields and farmlands, and an apple orchard as well as a forested hillside. The Eastern Highway ran by the front door.

Melville's father-in-law loaned him $3000 toward the purchase of the place. Melville also carried a mortgage which he felt he could easily repay as an important and successful author. This would prove to be a burden to him in the years to come.

Built by Captain David Bush Pittsfield's first town clerk, a part-time banker and part-time farmer between 1783 and 1786, the house is not a typical New England farmhouse. The rooms are large and the ceilings high. It is constructed on a central chimney which not only supported the physical structure but also provided heat to all of the principal rooms with three open fireplaces on each of the two main floors. Bush sold the property, which he may have also used as a tavern and an inn, to Dr. Brewster in 1844; six years later it became the Melville family residence.

In a letter to his friend Evert Duychinck in December of 1859 Melville wrote: *"I have a sort of sea-feeling here in the country... My room seems a ship's cabin; and at nights when I wake up and hear the winds shrieking, I almost fancy there is too much sial on the house, and I had better go on the roof and rig the chimney."*

When Melville decided in 1851 to farm the land he plowed the north meadow and uncovered a great many Indian artifacts which inspired the name "Arrowhead" for the place. It was his principle home for the next thirteen years until 1863 when he surrendered it to his brother Allan Melville in exchange for a house on the east side of Manhattan where the author moved with his wife and four children, three of whom had been born at Arrowhead. The decision to move was a financial one for Melville. He needed to find a job to support his large family. He was pleased that his own brother could take the place for it meant he could return periodically to relive some of his best times, but it was a sad and bitter occasion when his carriage pulled away from the elegant, curved driveway to the south of the home he had come to cherish.

Melvilles remained in possession of the property, now diminished in scope due to sales of tracts of property to raise money on which the Melville family lived, until 1927 when Herman's elderly nieces finally sold the house at auction and left the ancestral home (77 years of Melville occupancy made it so). His final book of poems offer many recollections of this place which inspired some of his finest work in fiction and poetry. The Berkshire County Historical Society purchased the house in 1974 and opened it as a museum dedicated to Herman Melville in 1975.

BERKSHIRE HISTORICAL SOCIETY
AT
HERMAN MELVILLE'S
ARROWHEAD

Visit us at www.mobydick.org
413.442.1793
Look for other titles at www.melvillepress.com

J. Peter Bergman is the Director of Communications and Community Relations for the Berkshire County Historical Society at Herman Melville's Arrowhead. He is the author of countless newspaper and magazine articles, theater, art and book reviews and several books including the Charles Dickens Award winning collection of short short fiction, *Counterpoints*, and the novel *Small Ironies*.

CPSIA information can be obtained at www.ICGtesting.com
Printed in the USA
BVOW02s1921050216

435729BV00001B/5/P